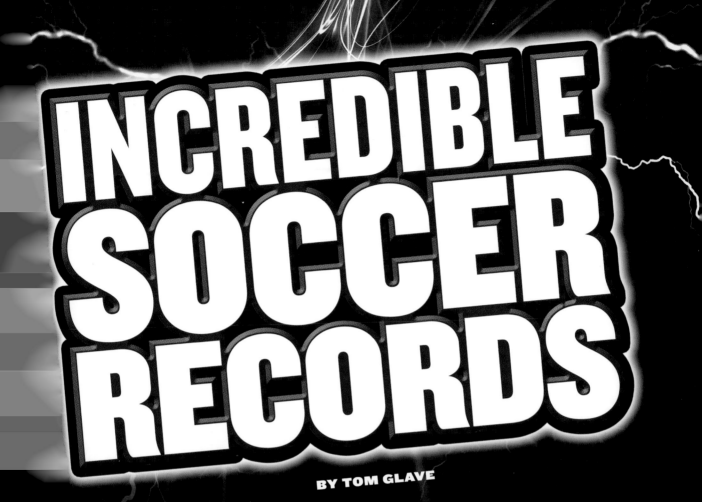

INCREDIBLE SOCCER RECORDS

BY TOM GLAVE

Published by The Child's World®
1980 Lookout Drive • Mankato, MN 56003-1705
800-599-READ • www.childsworld.com

Acknowledgments
The Child's World®: Mary Swensen, Publishing Director
Red Line Editorial: Editorial direction and production
The Design Lab: Design

Photographs ©: Shutterstock Images, cover, 1, 2, 23; Photo Works/Shutterstock
Images, 5; Robin Alam/ISI/Corbis, 6; AP Images, 9; Daily Mirror/Mirrorpix/Corbis, 10;
Julian Stratenschulte/dpa/Corbis, 13; Darryl Dyck/The Canadian Press/AP Images,
14; Manu Fernandez/AP Images, 17; Kimimasa Mayama/Reuters/Corbis, 18;
Maurizio Borsari/AFLO/Nippon News/Corbis, 19; Imaginechina/Corbis, 20

Design Element: Shutterstock Images

ISBN 9781503808911
LCCN 2015958449

Printed in the United States of America
Mankato, MN
June, 2016
PA02307

TABLE OF CONTENTS

CHAPTER 1
U.S. Records...4

CHAPTER 2
World Cup Records...8

CHAPTER 3
Women's Records...12

CHAPTER 4
International Records...16

GLOSSARY...22

TO LEARN MORE...23

INDEX...24

ABOUT THE AUTHOR...24

MOST CAREER MLS GOALS
MOST CAREER MLS ASSISTS
Landon Donovan
144 Goals, 136 Assists

Landon Donovan holds two big records in Major League Soccer (MLS). He scored 144 goals during his 14 seasons. Donovan broke the MLS career record in 2014. Jeff Cunningham had the old record. Cunningham retired in 2011 with 134 goals.

Donovan also has the most **assists** in MLS history. He set that record in 2014 as well. His pass helped teammate Robbie Keane score a goal. MLS named an award after Donovan. It goes to the league's most valuable player (MVP). Each year, that great player now wins the Landon Donovan MVP Award.

LANDON DONOVAN

HERBALIFE

BIGGEST U.S. CROWD
109,318 People
Manchester United vs. Real Madrid
August 2, 2014

The University of Michigan always draws huge crowds for its home football games. Michigan Stadium also hosted the largest crowd to watch a soccer match in the United States. The match was between two of the world's most popular teams. Manchester United beat Real Madrid 3–1 in front of 109,318 fans. The match was part of a preseason tournament.

LONGEST MLS WINNING STREAK

15 Games

Los Angeles Galaxy, 1997-98

The Los Angeles Galaxy won their last six games of the 1997 season. That helped them get into the playoffs. The next season, the Galaxy won their first nine games. Their first win of the 1998 season came on **penalty kicks**. The Galaxy scored 31 goals during those nine wins. The streak ended with a loss to the Chicago Fire in May.

TOUGH D

Real Salt Lake had a great defense in 2010. The team allowed 20 goals in 30 games. That is the fewest goals allowed in one season in MLS history. Keeper Nick Rimando had 14 shutouts and made 78 saves. A strong defense in front of him stopped teams from taking shots.

CHAPTER 2

WORLD CUP RECORDS

MOST GOALS IN A WORLD CUP

13 Goals

Just Fontaine, France • 1958

Just Fontaine did not know he would play in the 1958 World Cup. Then an injury to a teammate opened a spot for Fontaine. He certainly took advantage of the opportunity. Fontaine scored in all six matches France played. He started with a **hat trick** in his first game. He finished with a four-goal game as France took third place.

MOST CHAMPIONSHIPS
3 Championships
Pelé, Brazil • 1958, 1962, 1970

Pelé became famous around the world as a teenager. He was 17 when he helped Brazil win the World Cup in 1958. Pelé is the youngest player to score at the World Cup. He had a hat trick in the 1958 semifinals. He also scored in the final. He went on to lead Brazil to two more titles. No other player has won the World Cup more than twice.

GEOFF HURST

MOST GOALS IN A FINAL
3 Goals
Geoff Hurst, England • 1966

England won the 1966 World Cup on its home turf. Geoff Hurst scored three times in the final to clinch the victory. He is the only man with a hat trick in the World Cup final.

Hurst scored his first goal early in the game against West Germany. But the West Germans scored late to tie the game 2–2 and force **extra time**. Hurst scored in the 101st minute to give England the lead. His goal bounced straight down off the crossbar. To this day, many fans argue the goal should not have counted. Hurst scored again in the final minute to give England a 4–2 victory.

FASTEST GOAL
11 Seconds
Hakan Şükür, Turkey • 2002

Hakan Şükür scored only one goal in the 2002 World Cup. But it helped Turkey beat South Korea for third place. It also set a record. South Korea started the match with the ball. Şükür intercepted a bad pass to South Korea's back line. He quickly shot it. The ball slipped past a surprised keeper. The game was just 11 seconds old.

BRAZIL'S BIG STADIUM

Brazil built a stadium to host the 1950 World Cup. It could hold 200,000 people. Maracanã Stadium set a record when Uruguay beat Brazil 2–1 in the final. There were 173,850 tickets sold for the match. No soccer match has ever been played in front of that many fans. More people entered the stadium without tickets. It's believed that more than 200,000 people were in attendance.

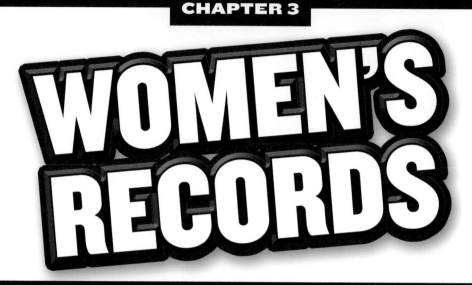

CHAPTER 3

WOMEN'S RECORDS

MOST CAREER INTERNATIONAL GOALS
184 Goals
Abby Wambach, USA

Abby Wambach has scored more goals in international competition than anyone in history. She scored at the Women's World Cup. She scored at the Olympics. She scored in **friendlies**.

Fellow U.S. forward Mia Hamm had the old record of 158 goals. Wambach broke that in 2013. She scored four times in one game to set the record.

Wambach scored one goal at the 2015 Women's World Cup. She retired at the end of the year with 184 career goals.

MOST CAREER WOMEN'S WORLD CUP GOALS
15 Goals
Marta, Brazil

Marta played in the Women's World Cup four times for Brazil. She scored 15 goals in those four tournaments. Marta set the record with a goal at the 2015 Women's World Cup in Canada. Germany's Birgit Prinz had the old record of 14.

Marta scored seven times at the 2007 World Cup. She won the award for most goals in that tournament. She was also named the FIFA Women's World Player of the Year a record five times.

MARTA

FASTEST WOMEN'S WORLD CUP HAT TRICK

16 Minutes

Carli Lloyd, USA • July 5, 2015

Carli Lloyd's three goals helped the United States win the 2015 Women's World Cup. It was the first hat trick in the Women's World Cup final. And it took her only 16 minutes to complete.

Lloyd scored in the third minute to give the USA an early lead against Japan. That was the fastest goal in a World Cup final. Then she scored again two minutes later. Finally, Lloyd stole the ball at **midfield** in the 16th minute. She saw the keeper was away from the goal. Lloyd took a long shot. The keeper raced back but could not get there in time.

CARLI LLOYD

LONGEST WOMEN'S WORLD CUP SHUTOUT STREAK

679 Minutes

Germany, 2003–2011

Germany used a strong defense to win the 2007 Women's World Cup. Nobody scored a goal on the Germans in their six games. The scoreless streak began as Germany won the 2003 Women's World Cup. It did not allow a goal in the last 57 minutes of that final. The streak ended at the 2011 tournament. Canada scored against Germany in the first game.

WATCHING THE WORLD CUP

The Rose Bowl in California was packed in 1999. The Women's World Cup final drew 90,185 fans. It was the biggest crowd to watch a women's soccer game. The home fans went home happy, too. The United States beat China on penalty kicks to win the title.

CHAPTER 4

INTERNATIONAL RECORDS

MOST CONSECUTIVE EUROPEAN CUP CHAMPIONSHIPS
5 Championships
Real Madrid • 1956–1960

In 1956 a newspaper in France had an idea for a tournament. The champions of the biggest leagues throughout Europe would play in it. They called the tournament the European Cup. Real Madrid won it the first five years. No other team has won more than three in a row. The tournament's name changed in 1992. It is now the Champions League. Real Madrid has won it a record 10 times.

MOST GOALS IN A CALENDAR YEAR
91 Goals
Lionel Messi • 2012

Lionel Messi played in 69 games in 2012. He played for his Spanish club team, FC Barcelona. He also played for the Argentina national team. He scored 91 goals in those 69 games. That beat the single-year record of 85. It had been set by Gerd Müller in 1972. Müller played for German club Bayern Munich and the West Germany national team.

Messi scored 79 goals for Barcelona and 12 goals for Argentina. He broke the record on December 9. He scored two goals in a Spanish league game against Real Betis.

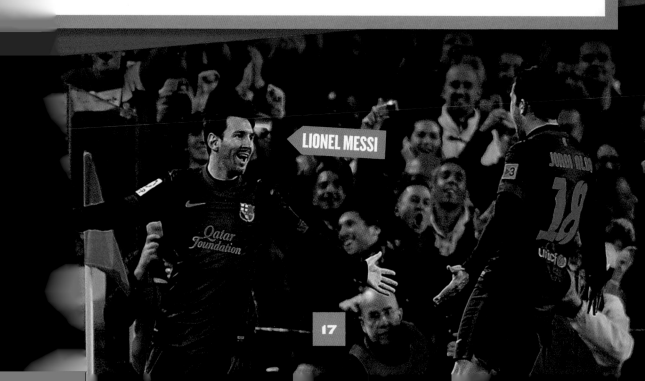

LIONEL MESSI

ALI DAEI

MOST CAREER INTERNATIONAL GOALS

109 Goals

Ali Daei, Iran

Ali Daei played for some strong club teams throughout Europe and Asia. But he did his best work for Iran's national team. Daei scored 109 goals in 149 games for Iran. No man has scored more goals in international play. Daei made his debut for Iran in 1993. He broke the old record in 2003. Daei passed Ferenc Puskás of Hungary with his 85th goal. The next year he scored four goals in a game against Laos. That included his 100th career goal. Daei scored his last goal for Iran in 2006.

MOST CAREER GOALS SCORED BY A KEEPER
129 Goals
Rogério Ceni, São Paulo FC and Brazil

The keeper is supposed to stop goals. But Rogério Ceni also scores them. Through 2015, Ceni had scored 129 goals for São Paulo FC. He began playing for the famous club in Brazil in 1990. Ceni doesn't kick the ball from one end of the field to the other when he scores. He takes all of São Paulo's free kicks and penalty kicks. He passed the old record of 62 goals in 2006.

ROGÉRIO CENI

ARCHIE THOMPSON

MOST GOALS BY A PLAYER IN ONE GAME
13 Goals
Archie Thompson, Australia • April 11, 2001

Australia set a record when it beat American Samoa 31–0 in 2001. No team had ever scored more goals in a World Cup **qualifier**. Archie Thompson scored a record 13 goals that day. He scored eight times before halftime. Thompson broke a record that was 93 years old. Sophus Nielsen scored 10 times for Denmark in the 1908 Olympics.

American Samoa was not playing its best players that day. Many team members had problems with their passports and could not travel. The U.S. island territory had to use teenagers from its youth team.

MOST GOALS BY A TEAM IN ONE GAME
149 Goals
AS Adema vs. Stade Olympique
October 31, 2002

Stade Olympique lost a game in the Madagascar national tournament. The players blamed the referee. So to protest, the team lost its next game on purpose. It scored 149 **own goals**. The players scored goals for the other team to show they were upset.

Stade Olympique got in trouble after the match. Four players and the coach were punished.

WHO'S THE KING?

Some records are in dispute. Guinness World Records says Pelé has the most goals in a career. He scored 1,279 goals in 1,363 games. But some historians believe the record belongs to Josef Bican. He was credited with 1,468 goals in 918 games. Bican played in Austria and Czechoslovakia from 1931 to 1956.

GLOSSARY

assists (uh-SISTS): Assists are passes that help a teammate score. Landon Donovan holds the MLS record for most assists.

extra time (EK-struh TIME): Extra time is added to a game to determine a winner if the score is tied. West Germany and England played extra time in the 1966 World Cup final.

friendlies (FREND-leez): Friendlies are games that are not played as part of a league schedule or tournament. Abby Wambach scored goals in the Olympics, the Women's World Cup, and in friendlies.

hat trick (HAT TRIK): A hat trick occurs when one player scores three goals in a game. Pelé had a hat trick in the 1958 World Cup semifinals.

keeper (KEE-pur): Short for "goalkeeper," the keeper is the player who protects the team's goal. Carli Lloyd beat the keeper with a shot from midfield in the 2015 Women's World Cup Final.

midfield (MID-feeld): Midfield is the center area of the field. Carli Lloyd stole the ball at midfield before her long goal against Japan.

own goals (OHN GOHLS): Own goals are scored by a player against his or her own team, usually by mistake. A team from Madagascar intentionally scored 149 own goals in one game.

penalty kicks (PEN-uhl-tee KIKS): Penalty kicks are one-on-one shots with a player against a keeper. The United States beat China in penalty kicks to win the 1999 Women's World Cup.

qualifier (KWAHL-uh-fye-ur): A qualifier is a game that helps a team get into a tournament. Australia scored 31 goals in one World Cup qualifier.

IN THE LIBRARY

Gifford, Clive. *The Inside Story of Soccer*. New York: Rosen Central, 2012.

Jökulsson, Illugi. *Stars of Women's Soccer*. New York: Abbeville Press Publishers, 2015.

Rausch, David. *Major League Soccer*. Minneapolis, MN: Bellwether Media, 2015.

ON THE WEB

Visit our Web site for links about soccer: **childsworld.com/links**

Note to Parents, Teachers, and Librarians: We routinely verify our Web links to make sure they are safe and active sites. So encourage your readers to check them out!

INDEX

Bican, Josef, 21

Cahill, Tim, 4
Ceni, Rogério, 19
Cunningham, Jeff, 5

Daei, Ali, 18
Donovan, Landon, 5

Fontaine, Just, 8

Hamm, Mia, 12
Hurst, Geoff, 10

Keane, Robbie, 5

Lloyd, Carli, 14

Marta, 13
Messi, Lionel, 17
Müller, Gerd, 17

Nielsen, Sophus, 10

Pelé, 9, 21
Prinz, Birgit, 13
Puskás, Ferenc, 18

Rimando, Nick, 7

Şükür, Hakan, 11

Thompson, Archie, 20

Wambach, Abby, 12

ABOUT THE AUTHOR

Tom Glave learned to write about sports at the University of Missouri. He has written about sports for newspapers in New Jersey, Missouri, Arkansas, and Texas. He has also written several books about sports.